Berkshire

Edited By Megan Roberts

First published in Great Britain in 2019 by:

Young Writers
Remus House
Coltsfoot Drive
Peterborough
PE2 9BF
Telephone: 01733 890066
Website: www.youngwriters.co.uk

Book Design by Spencer Hart

SB ISBN 978-1-78988-430-2
Printed and bound in the UK by BookPrintingUK
Website: www.bookprintinguk.com
YB0402E

Foreword

Dear Reader,

Are you ready to explore the wonderful delights of poetry?

Young Writers' *Poetry Patrol* gang set out to encourage and ignite the imaginations of 5-7 year-olds as they took their first steps into the magical world of poetry. With **Riddling Rabbit**, **Acrostic Croc** and **Sensory Skunk** on hand to help, children were invited to write an acrostic, sense poem or riddle on any theme, from people to places, animals to objects, food to seasons. *Poetry Patrol* is also a great way to introduce children to the use of poetic expression, including onomatopoeia and similes, repetition and metaphors, acting as stepping stones for their future poetic journey.

All of us here at Young Writers believe in the importance of inspiring young children to produce creative writing, including poetry, and we feel that seeing their own poem in print will keep that creative spirit burning brightly and proudly.

We hope you enjoy reading this wonderful collection as much as we enjoyed reading all the entries.

Contents

EP Collier Primary School, Reading

Fir Tree Primary School & Nursery, Newbury

Hilltop First School, Windsor

LVS, Ascot

St John's Beaumont School, Old Windsor

The Poems

Spring Babies

C utest creatures in the land,
U nder trees, the creatures leap,
T ell them please, there's no more food!
E ating juicy, orange carrots.

B abies, these creatures are,
U nder trees these animals are born,
N o, please don't harm them!
N one of these creatures live in the cold,
I n spring, new animals are born.
E ating healthy, good vegetables,
S inging squeaky tunes.

Sofia Ensell (7)

All Saints Infants School, Reading

Fireworks

F ireworks as hot as the sun, they glow in the sky.
I see the fireworks so bright up high,
R ight in the sky, fireworks are shooting quickly.
E veryone is screaming for more and more.
W hooshing in the sky, fireworks are shooting,
O range fireworks are shooting in the air.
R ight up, everybody looks at the fireworks,
K ids look at the fireworks for ages.
S oon, the fireworks go down.

Eshal Amin (6)
All Saints Infants School, Reading

Elysha's Sweet Land

E lysha had an idea, she was going to build Elysha
L and. So, come and help her. All your favourite sweets are there so
Y ou can come and join her in her world.
S weets are free. Homes are made of sweets and chocolates.
H ouses are made out of things like
A pples, Twix, Coca-Cola, blueberries, sweets and chewy bubblegum!

Elysha Sarah Fordjour (7)
All Saints Infants School, Reading

Winter Babies

B est animal on Earth,
A rctic animals these can be.
B eneath the world, is where they live.
Y ou probably think they are the cutest
animals on Earth.

F urry they are,
O wls they eat,
X -ray eyes.
E verybody thinks they're cute.
S lugs they eat.

Frankie Evans (7)
All Saints Infants School, Reading

Winter

W inter is as cold as ice,
I t's always cold in winter, but the exciting part is the snow.
N ow, it's time to play in the snow.
T he snow is good for snowmen.
E ating ice on the snow,
R eally cold, it's time to go.

Jessica Sood (7)
All Saints Infants School, Reading

Acrostics

A crostics are the world of a dream,
C ramped inside your brain,
R ude ones, nice ones and funny ones,
O nes that are great.
S ome are funny,
T iny ones,
I am like a riddle,
C ramped inside your brain.

Henry Woodhouse (6)
All Saints Infants School, Reading

What Am I?

I am nothing right now,
MPs say no to my plan.
I am at 10 Downing Street and the House of Commons.
The exit day is March 29th, Friday.
There is one month left.
What am I?

Answer: Brexit.

Malachi Ngoni (7)
All Saints Infants School, Reading

Magic Unicorns

Unicorns don't taste that good,
Unicorns smell really good.
Unicorns look so pretty,
Unicorns feel really fluffy.
Unicorns are the best,
Unicorns sound really quiet.

Abia Shabaz Hussain Akhtar (7)
All Saints Infants School, Reading

What Am I?

I am soft and smooth.
I am as soft as a zebra.
I can be black and white.
I am smaller than a table.
I come from England.
What am I?

Answer: A snake.

Kai Makepeace (5)
All Saints Infants School, Reading

What Am I?

I am blue and green,
I eat green grass.
I am as big as a parrot,
I am as colourful as a rainbow.
I live in India.
What am I?

Answer: A peacock.

Nahrelle Toyen Collins (5)
All Saints Infants School, Reading

What Am I?

I have a clever nose,
I sleep in trees,
I am black and white,
I live in forests in China,
I eat delicious bamboo.
What am I?

Answer: A panda.

Harry Jack Pumphrey (6)
All Saints Infants School, Reading

What Am I?

I am green and bumpy
I have a long tail,
I live in rivers.
I have sharp, large teeth,
I have a curved mouth.
What am I?

Answer: A crocodile.

Connor Swift (5)
All Saints Infants School, Reading

What Am I?

I live in a forest far away,
I have a long mane,
I look like a horse,
I have wings,
I have a shiny horn.
What am I?

Answer: A unicorn.

Lyla Wright (6)
All Saints Infants School, Reading

What Am I?

I have a long neck,
I have a tail,
I live by a volcano,
I can fly high,
I breathe fire.
What am I?

Answer: A dragon.

Noah Brown (6)
All Saints Infants School, Reading

What Am I?

I can fly,
I am as big as a balloon,
I am red and yellow and blue.
I have a pointy beak.
What am I?

Answer: A parrot.

Alfie Cook (6)

All Saints Infants School, Reading

What Am I?

I have a horn,
I can fly,
I have magic,
I have hooves,
I have a mane.
What am I?

Answer: A unicorn.

Bridget Hope Derrett (5)
All Saints Infants School, Reading

What Am I?

I can be any colour,
I have wings,
I live in the clouds,
I have a horn.
What am I?

Answer: A unicorn.

Emma Ensell (5)
All Saints Infants School, Reading

Cats

C ats drink milk,
A nd cats lick their fur.
"T ee hee," some cats say that.
S ee! A cat!

Kamsi Onyeka (5)
All Saints Infants School, Reading

Who Am I?

I am big,
I have false teeth,
I have grey hair,
I have some family.
Who am I?

Answer: The Queen.

Harry Grant (6)
All Saints Infants School, Reading

What Am I?

I am an animal with four legs.
I live in the Arctic.
I am hibernating now.
What am I?

Answer: A fox.

Jacob How (6)
All Saints Infants School, Reading

What Am I?

I am something that flies in the sky,
I have wings,
I have a beak.
What am I?

Answer: A bird.

Mark Akor (6)
All Saints Infants School, Reading

What Am I?

I am stripy,
I am rough,
I bite people,
I have sharp claws.
What am I?

Answer: A tiger.

Yusuf Luqman Kayani (7)
All Saints Infants School, Reading

Who Am I?

I'm green,
I ruined Christmas,
I have a dog called Max.
Who am I?

Answer: The Grinch.

Jess Robinson (7)
All Saints Infants School, Reading

What Am I?

I am fluffy and rough,
I have nice, fluffy ears.
I am scared.
What am I?

Answer: A dog.

Charlie De La Warr (6)
All Saints Infants School, Reading

Silly Snakes

S illy snakes,
N ame is Sam.
A nswers,
K ing cobra,
E ating.

Sebastian Whitty (5)

All Saints Infants School, Reading

What Am I?

I am an animal,
I live in the sea.
I eat things from the sea floor.
I am as big as a hamster.

Ella Gregory (6)
All Saints Infants School, Reading

Bedtime

B ig house in town,
E ating pies,
D inners are yummy.

Cooper Arthurs (7)
All Saints Infants School, Reading

What Am I?

I live in a factory,
I'm half-pet and half-robot,
It is tricky to pronounce my name.
My enemies are dogs or puppies,
You can change my language to something different.
I even have settings,
I am puppet-sized.
What am I?

Answer: A Tamagotchi.

David Stratulat (6)
Bearwood Primary School, Sindlesham

The Fast Things

I am as fast as lightning,
I am flat and light,
I race as quick as anything.
I am a Nintendo Star!
I am slick and funny,
You can do anything with me
And I run as fast as a cheetah with your help.
What am I?

Answer: A Nintendo Mii.

Toby Smith (6)
Bearwood Primary School, Sindlesham

The Awesome Driver!

Toby taught me to drive,
I am funny with games,
I have circle hands,
I feel hard things like hammers hammering heavily,
I'm co-head of Mario Mii Land,
I taste cool, awesome and amazing things.
Who am I?

Answer: Special Mii, Noah.

Noah Smith (6)
Bearwood Primary School, Sindlesham

The Scary Pinchers

I am as red as the juiciest red apple in the world.
I am as scary as a growling, roaring tiger.
I have claws as sharp as knives.
I can swim,
I have six feet,
People are nervous of me.
What am I?

Answer: A lobster.

Ojas Shah (7)
Bearwood Primary School, Sindlesham

The Big Reds

I wear a red kit,
I am in the Six Nations and rankings
I am a sport.
My team weight is 891,
I am a big team,
I am a muscly team.
I am as fast as lightning.
What am I?

Answer: The Welsh Rugby Team.

Thomas Henry Burke-Davies (7)
Bearwood Primary School, Sindlesham

The Icy Wheel

I am light brown,
I am delicious to eat,
I am squidgy like a chocolate cake.
I'm as squashy as a squashy ball.
I roll away faster than a car,
I am like a wheel.
What am I?

Answer: A doughnut.

Mihika Sharma (7)
Bearwood Primary School, Sindlesham

The Sprinkles

I have a hole in the middle,
I am tasty and delicious,
I am round and smooth,
I don't always have sprinkles,
I am sticky,
I have lots of sugar.
What am I?

Answer: A doughnut.

Simar Bhutani (7)
Bearwood Primary School, Sindlesham

What Am I?

I am bright
I am magical
I am beautiful
I am a type of fish
I make wishes come true
I am very kind
I am not edible
I am colourful.
What am I?

Answer: A flounder.

Param Shah (7)
Bearwood Primary School, Sindlesham

The Numbers

I have numbers on me,
I go like this: *tick, tock!*
I'm on the wall,
I can go on your hand,
I have two arrows,
I tell you something.
What am I?

Answer: A clock.

Poppy Sue Johnson (7)
Bearwood Primary School, Sindlesham

A Challenging Riddle

You can write on me inside,
You have lines on me,
I can be any colour,
You can buy me from a shop,
You can sometimes rip pages out of me.
What am I?

Answer: A book.

Gia Gill (6)
Bearwood Primary School, Sindlesham

Strong Animals

People are scared of me,
I am fierce,
I have a tail.
I have tough and rough teeth,
I am a type of dinosaur,
Kids have books of me.
What am I?

Answer: A T-rex.

Kirk Boadu (6)
Bearwood Primary School, Sindlesham

The Monkey

I swing from the branches
I am cheeky
I like playing with people
I live in the jungle
I am as cheeky as a person.
What am I?

Answer: A monkey.

Liam James Toop (7)

Bearwood Primary School, Sindlesham

Slithering

I am slimy,
I am poisonous,
I have spots on me.
I am strong,
I am squishy,
I can get brand new skin.
What am I?

Answer: A snake.

Logan Alexander Karagiannakis (7)
Bearwood Primary School, Sindlesham

The Noisy Animal

I have a thick mane
I am loud
I have sharp claws
I am big
I have four legs
I have a bushy tail.
What am I?

Answer: A lion.

Tilly Kristiana Rogers (7)
Bearwood Primary School, Sindlesham

What Am I?

I have horns
I am strong
I am grey and black
I have two letters in my name
I am a big fighter.
What am I?

Answer: An ox.

Finlay James Gee (7)
Bearwood Primary School, Sindlesham

Underwater Mystery

I am half-human and half-fish,
I have scales on my tail,
I live in the sea,
I never go on land.
What am I?

Answer: A mermaid.

Chloe Humphrey (7)
Bearwood Primary School, Sindlesham

A Flying Wing

I'm part of Star Wars,
I'm soft,
I'm playful,
I'm cute,
I'm helpful.
What am I?

Answer: A Porg.

Alex Smith (6)
Bearwood Primary School, Sindlesham

The Slithery Animal

I am slidey
I stick my tongue out
I sometimes have spots on me
I live in the jungle
What am I?

Answer: A snake.

Mia Griffin (6)
Bearwood Primary School, Sindlesham

Pretty Rings

I am round,
I am sparkly,
I am kind of flat,
I am yummy,
I look delicious.
What am I?

Answer: A doughnut.

Miley Smith (7)
Bearwood Primary School, Sindlesham

The Slither

I am very long,
I have patterns on me,
I can kill you.
I can send you to hospital.
What am I?

Answer: A snake.

Daniel James Makepeace (7)
Bearwood Primary School, Sindlesham

Winter

W inter is snowy, windy and icy
I cicles hang from snowy trees
N ice, snowy, icy cold winter.
T rees are covered with a blanket of snow,
you might get covered too, so wrap up
warm with your hood on.
E xciting, joyful presents to unwrap on
Christmas Day.
R ed robins chirping through the snowy
trees and jolly carol singers, making it so
much fun at Christmas time.

Theodore Leatham (6)
Crazies Hill CE Primary School, Wargrave

Winter Wonderland

W onderland, oh wonderful, fabulous
Wonderland,
I n and out, up and down, on the amazing,
great sledge ride.
N o one knows where Santa goes every day
and night.
T ucked up in bed, sleepy heads see the
little, shimmering snow and fall asleep.
E njoyable, exciting snow angels are made
in freezing cold snow.
R oaring cars are all stuck in the dirty,
mushy snow.

Annabel Rose Copland (7)
Crazies Hill CE Primary School, Wargrave

Wonderful Winter

W onderful winter, you sparkle so nicely,
I can smell the pungent fires,
N ice breezes blow through your hair,
T ingles go down my back when I play in
the snow.
E veryone goes to the big pond with their
skates,
R ows of elves make toys for girls and boys.

Martha Lowe (7)
Crazies Hill CE Primary School, Wargrave

Winter

I can see snow falling from the sky
and landing on my face.
I can smell hot chocolate
with marshmallows and cream.
I can hear jingling bells
on the Christmas tree.
I can taste roast turkey
and Christmas pudding.
I can feel presents wrapped up
in Santa wrapping paper.

Roberta Pope (6)

Crazies Hill CE Primary School, Wargrave

Wonderful Winter

I can see icy, shimmering flakes through the sky,
I can smell the smell of disgusting, pungent smoke from the fire,
I can hear the sound of hard hailstones crashing beneath my feet,
I can taste the miniature marshmallows in my hot chocolate,
I can feel the cold breeze hitting my face.

Yasmin Ingleby (7)

Crazies Hill CE Primary School, Wargrave

Lovely Snow

W onderful, beautiful, lovely snow,
I cy icicles hang from trees,
N asty, ferocious wind will blow the trees.
T ake your hat, scarf and gloves to school,
E xcited children open their presents,
R aging snow hits the ground quickly.

Keavie Rae Bush (7)

Crazies Hill CE Primary School, Wargrave

Snowy Winter

W onderful, cold winter,
I cy, freezing cold winter,
N ice, windy, slippery winter,
T ry eating amazing snow from out of the clouds.
E xciting winter is here,
R obins are naughty in winter and have red tummies!

Alexander James Ramsey (6)
Crazies Hill CE Primary School, Wargrave

Snow

W inter is fun because of snow showers.
I make a snow angel.
N oisy children scream with glee on sledges.
T rees have no leaves.
E verybody comes round to deliver Christmas presents.
R obins come out to sing.

Maisie Thatcher (5)
Crazies Hill CE Primary School, Wargrave

Winter

W hen wonderful, windy winter comes, you need to wrap up warm
I cicles hang from snowy trees
N ice winter wonderland
T asty hot chocolate reaches your tongue
E xciting winter
R obins are naughty in winter.

Ozzie Hopcroft (7)
Crazies Hill CE Primary School, Wargrave

Wonderful Winter

W onderful, windy winter,
I cicles hang from snowy trees,
N ice hot chocolate warming up your
tongue,
T remendous, terrific, slippery ice,
E xciting ice skating,
R obins are chirping around in winter.

Eddie James Copland (7)
Crazies Hill CE Primary School, Wargrave

Winter

W ondrous, wonderful, cold winter
I cy icicles come out at winter-time
N o one knows what Santa's grotto looks like
T errible snowstorms
E xciting, enjoyable Christmas
R emember Jesus.

Lilly Anne Young (7)
Crazies Hill CE Primary School, Wargrave

Storms

W onderful, cold winter,
I cy icicles hanging from the roof,
N asty snowstorms,
T winkly stars at night,
E veryone wrapped up warm,
R obins sing sweetly in the trees.

Hector Cyril Templeton (7)
Crazies Hill CE Primary School, Wargrave

Snowmen

W onderful windy winter,
I cicles hang from snowy trees,
N asty snowstorms,
T ime to put on the fire,
E xciting snowmen,
R eally exciting presents to open.

Seb Burton (7)
Crazies Hill CE Primary School, Wargrave

Winter

W onderful, windy winter
I cicles hang from snowy trees
N ice snowstorms
T he snow comes down quickly
E vil snowstorm frightens you
R aining snowflakes.

Megan Greenham (6)
Crazies Hill CE Primary School, Wargrave

Wondrous Winter

W ondrous, windy winter
I cy all around
N ever gets hot
T ingling icicles above
E vergreens still have leaves
R obins sing in the snowy trees.

Holly Davidson (7)
Crazies Hill CE Primary School, Wargrave

The Wintry Winter

I can hear icicles falling from the trees.
I can see everyone tucked up warmly
through the windows.
I can smell hot chocolate with
marshmallows.
I can feel the cold breeze around my ears.

Jason Bennett (5)
Crazies Hill CE Primary School, Wargrave

Senses In Winter

I can see white, sparkling snowflakes
I can hear people stepping in the crunchy snow
I can taste yummy hot chocolate
I can feel the cold wind
I can smell turkey in the oven.

Penelope Dunne (7)
Crazies Hill CE Primary School, Wargrave

Snow!

W onderful, snowy snow
I cy, frosty ice
N o one can see the grass
T he wonderful wind
E vil snowstorms
R ainy snowflakes.

Fox Drake (7)
Crazies Hill CE Primary School, Wargrave

Winter

W alking in the snow,
I n the snow, it is fun.
N ot hot.
T rees have no leaves,
E xciting!
R olling up snowballs.

Ben Webster (5)
Crazies Hill CE Primary School, Wargrave

The Alacorn Who Became A Princess

I wish I was a princess,
They have tiaras,
Shiny wings,
A bright horn
That's as beautiful as can be.
I just wish...
I just can't take it
I'm going to command it.
No, I can't, that's cheating.

Wait, what's happening?
Wings? A bright and beautiful horn,
As beautiful as can be
And a beautiful tiara,
Yippee!

Alyssa Jordan (6)
EP Collier Primary School, Reading

A Riddle Of A Not Real Animal

This animal is nice, lovely and bright.
It is not real and it's colourful.
It flies around but outside.
It's helpful and useful because it does magic.
It never cries and never lays eggs.
It gives birth to its babies.
It quietly talks and quickly runs around.
It's wonderful and it's like a pony or a horse.
It's kind and shiny.
It cannot walk.
It has a horn.
It jumps and doesn't fall over because it has wings.
It's always careful and never eats meat.
It doesn't like the cold so it doesn't like snow and winter.

It never gets muddy.
Santa Claus doesn't give it presents.
No one knows how it looks.
When it's a baby, it's a bit big.
It has a little horn when it's a baby.
Its eyes are always blue and it does not have eyelashes and eyebrows.
When it's an adult, it's always big.
What is it?

Answer: A unicorn.

Zoia Gryva (6)
EP Collier Primary School, Reading

Something Deep

It goes deeper and deeper.
Fish swim in it.
It starts with an 'O'.
There are plants inside and it's beautiful too.
It's a wonderful place - clean and fresh!
Splish, splash when people swim in it.
Quietly and calmly, the octopus goes.
Hungry sharks hunt for fish.
What is it?

Answer: The ocean.

Advika Badkur (7)
EP Collier Primary School, Reading

Spring

Spring is a season of joy,
In spring, you can touch plants,
In spring, you can smell plants,
In spring, you can hear plants.

Spring is a season of colours,
In spring, you can see rainbows,
In spring, you can see sunshine,
In spring, you can see colourful birds.

Aaiza Uzair (5)
EP Collier Primary School, Reading

Bella The Bunny

B ella the bunny has beauty all over her,
U sually, she goes on some adventures and she is very adventurous, but she is unbeatable.
N ew things she catches every day,
N ew things she catches for her play.
Y ou will be astonished by her soft, fluffy fur.

Simrah Merchant (7)
EP Collier Primary School, Reading

The Dragon

Do you like the dragon?
When he comes he gets wet
The dragon has big wings
"Go away you are very naughty.
Good boy, you are very good."
On the wing he is very silly
"No, you are very silly.
No, you are very scary."

Isha Seth (5)
EP Collier Primary School, Reading

Bush Masters

S neaking up on prey, getting closer and closer
N ice design on its back to disguise
A nd strikes like a lightning bolt
K eeping the life out of your brain
E ating your organs and being clever.

Isaac Holford (6)
EP Collier Primary School, Reading

A Rabbit

R abbits are hopping with joy
A s other animals are sleeping
B aby rabbits come out in spring
B y the soft, quiet, green meadow
I t's spring now!
T ime to say goodbye to winter

Kimora Simon (6)
EP Collier Primary School, Reading

Spring

S pring is coming,
P opping out, the blossoms come.
R ight up, the sun comes up.
I n spring, the sun comes up.
N o wind comes in spring,
G oing into spring is fun.

Evelyn Santos (6)

EP Collier Primary School, Reading

The Secret Riddle

I am big and tall.
There are different kinds of me.
I sometimes eat only meat or only plants.
I've existed already.
I am scary and sneaky.
What am I?

Answer: A dinosaur.

Shriyans Iyengar (6)
EP Collier Primary School, Reading

Snake

S nakes are really shimmery,
N ew poisonous snakes came from the sand,
A nts do not eat snakes.
K angaroos are bigger than snakes,
E veryone is scared of snakes!

Samuel John Cassidy (6)
EP Collier Primary School, Reading

Living With Lions

L iving with lions is fun and scary
I hope I treat them well or else
O n the third day, I will leave
N obody wants to take me out of the cage,
I might get out or not...

John (6)
EP Collier Primary School, Reading

The Riddle

It lives under the sea
It eats fish
It swims
It has a hard back
It carries its home everywhere
It is slow
It is big.
What is it?

Answer: A turtle.

Alfie Bignell (7)
EP Collier Primary School, Reading

A Snake

The snake is slithery and slimy
The snake has green skin
The snake is smelly
The snake is big
The snake is long
The snake is slimy and long
The snake is sparkly.

Divik Gupta (6)
EP Collier Primary School, Reading

What Am I?

I am running fast.
I have cubs.
I am spotty with nice eyes.
I am nice.
I'm fast to catch prey and I am helpful.
What am I?

Answer: A cheetah.

Alfie James Seymour (6)
EP Collier Primary School, Reading

Snake Acrostic

S lither and slither,
N o going near the snake
A s the snake can gobble you up,
K ids cannot go near the snake,
E ven when they love it.

Adam Kazi (6)
EP Collier Primary School, Reading

Spring

S now is gone,
P lants are growing,
R abbits are hopping,
I love this season,
N ew flowers are blooming,
G one is winter!

Pavel Svoboda (5)
EP Collier Primary School, Reading

Rabbit And Bunny

The rabbit and the bunny hopped and hopped,
All the way home,
"Nice bunny, little bunny," said the rabbit,
He wanted to do a lullaby,
Happily ever after!

Edel Saoirse Ricau (5)
EP Collier Primary School, Reading

Horses

H orses can neigh very well
O n the horse is fur which is very puffy
R eady to jump
S ee a horse on a farm
E verybody loves horses.

Kezia McKay (6)
EP Collier Primary School, Reading

The Person With A Red Coat

He is very good.
Every Christmas, every night, he gives toys to children,
He has eight reindeer.
Who is he?

Answer: Santa.

Zayaan Mirza (5)
EP Collier Primary School, Reading

Cars

Cars are fast,
Sometimes cars have to go slow,
When the red light comes on, we have to stop our car,
When the green light comes on, we can go!

Lucas Ramos (5)
EP Collier Primary School, Reading

What Is It?

Eats food off my feet.
Hungry, hungry.
Soft yellow feathers.
Spiky scratchy toes.
What is it?

Answer: A chicken.

Julio Narcis (7)
EP Collier Primary School, Reading

Snake

S lithery snake
N ecessary snake
A lways moving
K iller snake is disgusting
E ven smellier.

Trey-Junior Hyman-Davis (6)
EP Collier Primary School, Reading

Snake

The slithery snake is slithering
He slithers all over.
A snake is cool,
King snakes have stripes.
Everyone has a snake.

Archie Bartle (6)
EP Collier Primary School, Reading

A Scary Beast

It roars out loudly.
It has a long mane.
It has very sharp teeth.
What is it?

Answer: A lion.

Aylan Dello (7)
EP Collier Primary School, Reading

Dangerous Dragons

Dragons are dangerous
Really hot fire
Always coming from his mouth.

Theo (5), Yassine Halwes, Raul Stefan Diaconu (5), Masigam & Nanaki Puri
EP Collier Primary School, Reading

My Friendly Monster

M onsters are extendable and furry, also gigantic
O ne dangerous and aggressive creature
N aughty monsters always go, "Do, do, do!"
S illy monsters always go, "Boo!"
T iny creatures always sneak up on people and giggle a lot
E xcited monsters always have so much fun.
R ough monsters always play rough.

Riley John Cotter (6)
Fir Tree Primary School & Nursery, Newbury

The Friendly Monster

M assive, happy and scary monsters in the world
O ld with mega mummies to eat on Mondays
N oisy, naughty, nosy monsters in the world
S wift with green and black spots
T errifying and angry monsters
E xcited but worried with lots and lots of yellow spots
R oaming and making friends.

Gregory Peter Rosewarne (7)
Fir Tree Primary School & Nursery, Newbury

The Colourful Monster

M assive, munching, bellowing and
disgusting
O ne aggressive person and one disgusting
person
N asty and like the sound of a mammoth
lion and strange
S tranger that it is
T errified of people they see
E nvious and depressed and awful
R emove a person and a monster is super
grumpy.

Noor Mohamed (7)
Fir Tree Primary School & Nursery, Newbury

The Meagre Alien

A nnoying loud noises bellow from they sky
like the sound of lions
L ong noses on huge large faces
I mpressive, large, disgusting eyes shining
like the twinkly stars
E xcitable people scared and sad because
of the bellowing noises
N ight turns as dark as black and they
come out of their homes.

Lola Holmes (7)
Fir Tree Primary School & Nursery, Newbury

What Am I?

I am a mammoth-sized thing.
I'm sometimes very slimy.
I'm hairy too.
I can come out made of lava.
I am very frightening.
I have sharp fingernails.
I have sharp teeth.
I sometimes live in caves.
I sometimes have spikes.
What am I?

Answer: A mighty monster.

Daniel Freeman (6)
Fir Tree Primary School & Nursery, Newbury

The Good Alien

Aliens are silly but some are not.
Lots of aliens are good and bad.
Some aliens are happy, some are sad.
Aliens are as green as grass.
Some are black and some are white.
Aliens are a type of monster.
Some aliens are nasty and scary.

Sam Kamra (6)
Fir Tree Primary School & Nursery, Newbury

What Am I?

I am disgusting and green like a slimy swamp.
I live on the moon in space.
I eat filthy blue cheese.
I have a bright red spaceship.
I have curly dangly eyes.
What am I?

Answer: A grizzly alien.

Isla Barville (6)
Fir Tree Primary School & Nursery, Newbury

The Silly Monster

The silly monster is as silly as a clown.
He is as green as grass.
He is as colossal as a big towel.
He is dangerous and furry.

Alexandra Ghinea (6)

Fir Tree Primary School & Nursery, Newbury

What Is He?

He sleeps upside down in the wardrobe.
He likes to eat blood, bugs and bones.
He says, "Boo!"
He hides under people's beds.
What is he?

Answer: A scary monster.

Lily-May Fisher (6)
Fir Tree Primary School & Nursery, Newbury

What Is He?

He smells like mud and slugs.
He is very scary.
He is very noisy.
He has red eyes.
He is horrible with sharp teeth.
What is he?

Answer: A scary monster.

Dylan Knight (6)
Fir Tree Primary School & Nursery, Newbury

What Am I?

I have very smelly feet.
I live in a rock cave.
I like to eat bugs and rats.
I love animal soup.
What am I?

Answer: A scary monster.

Jessie Cuddihy-Oakes (6)
Fir Tree Primary School & Nursery, Newbury

A Special Vehicle

It looks big.
It carries people.
It stops at stations.
Its colour is red.
It has four wheels.
It has stairs.
It has lots of windows.
What is it?

Answer: A red bus.

Zihan Sebastian Zhang (6)
Hilltop First School, Windsor

Pirates

P irates here, pirates there
I like pirates to be everywhere
R obbing chests and digging up treasure
A rrr! This gives them much pleasure
T iptoe along when dark at night
E yepatch and cutlass sure to give a fright.

Oliver Gamble (6)
LVS, Ascot

Hedgehogs

The hedgehogs shuffle through the leaves,
blown gently by the breeze.
The hedgehog is covered in spines ever so prickly,
that cover his body ever so thickly.
When hedgehogs curl into a ball,
they look ever so small.

Layla McKee (6)
LVS, Ascot

A Busy Bee

I'm a bee and I do sting
I'm a bee and I can sing
I buzz all day and buzz all night
I make honey for my hive.

Arnav Pankhania (6)
LVS, Ascot

Harvest Poem

Apples, pears, plums
All grow on trees
They are lovely to eat
And all very sweet.

Lucas Guy Allen (6)
LVS, Ascot

My Magic Box

Based on 'The Magic Box' by Kit Wright

I will put in my box my mum's biggest smile
and the biggest roller coaster in the world.

I will put in my box the cutest penguin and
the feel of a squishy gummy bear.

I will put in my box a splash of a huge wave
in America.

My box will be made of gold and penguin
skin.

Joshua Okey-Nzewuihe (7)
St John's Beaumont School, Old Windsor

The Magic Box

Based on 'The Magic Box' by Kit Wright

I will put in the box a grassy savannah and
a splashy waterfall.

I will put in the box a splash of a huge wave
and a water splash volcano.

I will put in the box a huge Haribo that is as
big as the world and a white fluffy
Labrador.

I will put in the box a giant desert and a
giant football stadium for my family.

My box will be made from a grassy green
wave.

Jack Collacott (7)
St John's Beaumont School, Old Windsor

The Magic Box

Based on 'The Magic Box' by Kit Wright

I will put in my box a dragon's fire-breathing
breath and the smell of fresh mint.
I will put in my magic box the taste of fruity
Mentos and the beautiful Northern Lights.
I will put in my box a flying squeaking
mouse and three magic wishes.
My box is going to be made of gold and
metal.

Timur Shestakov (7)

St John's Beaumont School, Old Windsor

My Magic Box

Based on 'The Magic Box' by Kit Wright

I will put in my box three magic wishes and
the taste of a delicious pizza.
I will put in my box the biggest roller coaster
in the world and the sound of an ice skating
penguin.
I will put in my box a very slimy frog and the
feel of a big squishy gummy bear.
My box will be made of gold!

Harry Reynolds (7)
St John's Beaumont School, Old Windsor

My Magic Box

Based on 'The Magic Box' by Kit Wright

I will put in my box the smell of fresh mints and the colourful Northern Lights as nice as a rainbow.

I will put in my box the shining star of Jesus Christ and an owl twit-twooing.

I will put in my box St John's Beaumont and my best friend, Joshua.

My box is made out of gold, a dragon's hair and bones from a human.

Dim Agunbiade (7)
St John's Beaumont School, Old Windsor

My Magic Box

Based on 'The Magic Box' by Kit Wright

I will put in my box
the feel of a smooth rock and the sound of an ice skating penguin.
I will put in my box
a clock that never ticks and the burning smell of fireballs.
I will put in my box
losing my first tooth and a singing bird.
My box will be made of fur, steel, gold, snakes' coils and a giant stone.

Rafe Woolf (6)

St John's Beaumont School, Old Windsor

My Magic Box

Based on 'The Magic Box' by Kit Wright

I will put in my box the feel of a big squishy
gummy bear and the colourful Northern
Lights.

I will put in my box a flying squeaking
mouse and the biggest roller coaster in the
world.

I will put in my box a blue erupting volcano
and my mum's smile.

My box is made out of colourful Lego bricks.

Raiyen Man (7)
St John's Beaumont School, Old Windsor

My Magic Box

Based on 'The Magic Box' by Kit Wright

I will put in my box a flying squealing mouse
and a whale splashing in water.

I will put in my box a hungry dragon and a
squishy penguin.

I will put in my box a snake with three heads
and a box that can talk.

Yiyang Sun (6)

St John's Beaumont School, Old Windsor

My Magic Box

Based on 'The Magic Box' by Kit Wright

I will put in my magic box my old nanny telling me a story and the sound of the burning sun.

I will put in my magic box laughing at my dad's jokes and my mum's smile.

I will put in my magic box three magic wishes and the colourful Northern Lights.

My box will be made of fur.

Oscar Hirai (6)
St John's Beaumont School, Old Windsor

Magic Box

Based on 'The Magic Box' by Kit Wright

I will put in my box the grassy savannah
and the colourful Northern Lights.

I will put in my box a hypnotised fly
and a pinch of soft silky sand.

I will put in my box a blue erupting ice
volcano.

My box will be made out of glass, diamonds
and coal.

Maxi Moston (7)
St John's Beaumont School, Old Windsor

The Magic Box

Based on 'The Magic Box' by Kit Wright

I will put in my box the grassy savannah and
the colourful Northern Lights.
I will put in my box shells that I have
collected on the beach.
I will put in my box colourful jewels.
I will put in my box the biggest most
colourful pizza.
My box will be made of bronze.

Stepan Reznik (6)
St John's Beaumont School, Old Windsor

My Magic Box

Based on 'The Magic Box' by Kit Wright

I will put in my box a dinosaur's first tooth
and the sound of water crashing against a
rock.
I will put in my box a spark from the loudest
firework and the fluffiest Labrador.
My box is made of blood.

Conor Healy (6)
St John's Beaumont School, Old Windsor

My Magic Box

Based on 'The Magic Box' by Kit Wright

I will put in my box a fiery spark redder than a ruby and a fiery eagle.
I will put in my box a clock that has no time and jewellery shinier than lightning.
I will put in my box a star blacker than a panther.
And my box will be made of ruby!

Elliot Lai-Cheong (6)
St John's Beaumont School, Old Windsor

My Magic Box

Based on 'The Magic Box' by Kit Wright

I will put in my box
the grassy savannah.
I will put in my box the beautiful
Northern Lights.
I will put in my box a blue erupting
ice volcano.
I will put in my box an earthquake.
My box is made out of snakeskin.

Harry Waterson (7)
St John's Beaumont School, Old Windsor

Young Writers Information

We hope you have enjoyed reading this book – and that you will continue to in the coming years.

If you're a young writer who enjoys reading and creative writing, or the parent of an enthusiastic poet or story writer, do visit our website **www.youngwriters.co.uk**. Here you will find free competitions, workshops and games, as well as recommended reads, a poetry glossary and our blog.

If you would like to order further copies of this book, or any of our other titles, then please give us a call or visit **www.youngwriters.co.uk**.

Young Writers
Remus House
Coltsfoot Drive
Peterborough
PE2 9BF
(01733) 890066
info@youngwriters.co.uk

 @YoungWritersUK  @YoungWritersCW